BookBaby Publishing
7905 N. Crescent Blvd.
Pennsauken, NJ 08110

info@bookbaby.com

Three Little Words
To Look At Things A Little Differently
copyright © 2020 by Terri "Lovie" Delaney

ISBN 978-1-09833-600-4

THE DOOR'S OPEN

COME ON IN

A Note from the Author

This little book of mine, I'm gonna let it shine...
Oops, there I go again, breaking out in a tune
playing in my head (insert smile!). In all
sincerity, this book is written to share with
and give you a much-needed break from all the
uncertain senselessness going on in our world.
We're all craving our own simplicity. We all wish
for things to be and stay calm. Let's ease up on
ourselves and hit the pause button for a bit.
Which is why and how this book has come to be.
When I started this, so many (and some not so
many) great words swirled around in my head
and my heart. I learned and changed a lot, all
for the better and, yes, with putting just
three little words together. I needed to find a
way to make things easier again for myself
and, now hopefully, for you as well.

There is no rhyme or reason on how the words
have been put onto the pages. Feel free to
start at the beginning, the end or randomly
pick a page and find anything that makes you
smile, think, remember, feel, laugh, and take a
breath...feelings that ignite your insides!

Sparkle yourselves up my friends! xoxo

I cannot go without acknowledging the few and fabulous people who believed in, and encouraged, me to write and show what words can do (the good, bad and ugly words, as well as some people linked with the words) if I'm being honest. If not for them, I may never have created this book that was in my heart and head for so very long. For that, I gratefully dedicate this to them (they know who they are 😊) and to all of you, the readers, who find joy in the little things, like "Three Little Words" (wink, wink).

And a very *HUGE* and *SPECIAL* shoutout goes to "Hubbles" - my love, my friend, my heart (and P.S. a fantastic photographer) - for his deep devotion and endless support and for loving me more when I least deserve it. (*I absolutely love you more!!!!*)

♥ ♥ ♥

HERE
WE GO...

Hello My Lovelies

How Are You

Short and Sweet

Share the Joy

Makes Me Laugh

Enjoy the Ride

The Jersey Shore

Embrace It All

Forget the Risk

Bunches and Bunches

An Afternoon Nap

Act and React

More Cheese Please

Can I Help

Stand Your Ground

Please Help Me

Forget the Hurt

Just One More

We Can Hope

I Like It

I Love It

Not a Fan

Please Shut Up

Go Away Please

Tell Me Again

Rum and Coke

Breath Fresh Air

Just Walk Away

You Are Enough

Don't Back Down

Less Ice Please

I Am Enough

Slow It Down

Warm and Fuzzy

Kiss My A*s

Smell the Flowers

My Heart Aches

I Miss You

I Miss Them

It Is Enough

Can We Talk

I'm Truly Sorry

Those Chubby Cheeks

On the Side

Your Loss Loser

Chocolate's My Friend

You Are Fabulous

Take It Easy

Be More Kind

Are You Kidding

Make It Easy

Blah Blah Blah

It's Been Fun

Just Say No

See You Later

I Did Not

That's Not Happening

Don't Give Up

Never Give Up

Your Day's Coming

HERE'S THE KEY
TO YOUR HAPPINESS
TAKE YOUR TURN
START RIGHT NOW
DREAM YOUR DREAMS
AS FLOWERS BLOOM

My Gracie Girl

Love of Rum

Wiggle It Away

Get Some Rest

Take the Time

Doesn't Take Much

Give It Away

I Value You

Baked M&M Cookies

I'm Getting There

Come with Me

It's Better Now

I've Got Goosebumps

Good Morning Sunshine

Stand by Me

It's Cuddle Time

Just Checking In

Are You Okay

Did She Really

Know the Difference

Off the Couch

You Are Brave

You Are Strong

I Can't Anymore

Everything is Better

Tata and Tootaloo

Pull the Trigger

Unf*ck Yourself Already

We Need Peace

Send the Letter

Give to Love

That's Really Great

What a Shame

What a Sham

Gone Too Soon

Forever and Always

One Last Kiss

One More Time

One More Chat

Always and Forever

It Was Me

Stars at Night

Cherish the Moment

Kiss the Girl

Kiss the Boy

Much Better Off

When in Doubt

Sprinkles and Sparkles

Coffee and Cream

Jiggles Wiggles Giggles

Lots of Sugar

Firepit Party Time

Light the Night

We All Stumble

Kittens and Puppies

My First Love

One and Only

Hugs and Kisses

I've Been Searching

Living the Dream

Can We Go

My Francini Banini

Never Say Never

Cool Beans Baby

Not My Circus

It's Right There

Just Stopping By

Pull the Plug

On My Nerves

Just Say It

Just Tell Me

You've Been Duped

I Feel Bad

You Deserve It

Up Yours As*hole

The Sun Sets

Think About It

Truth Be Told

It's So Over

Cheek to Cheek

No Reason Whatsoever

Let's Go Now

Not My Clowns

You Are Despicable

Hopeless to Hopeful

It's Your Choice

Recover and Discover

Brilliant and Beautiful

The Sun Rises

It's Totally You

Confront Your Feelings

Little by Little

Smooch the Baby

My Cuddle Bug

Fluffy Not Fat

Good for You

You are Adorable

Simple is Easy

Wish Hope Dream

Always Be Yourself

Smile Even Though

Nourish Your Life

Because I Can

Pay Yourself Generously

Okie Dokie Pokie

Anytime and Always

Your Feelings Matter

Autumn Leaves Falling

You're Allowed To

Blow a Kiss

Make a Wish

Because You Can

Love and Sunshine

Celebrate the Days

Savor the Smiles

Be a Blessing

Light Yourself Up

Lighten Your Load

Enjoy the Weekend

You'll Get Yours

Make a Difference

Miller Light Draft

Time to Unplug

Rock Your World

Have an Opinion

Sparkle and Shine

Soar Sky High

Speak Your Voice

Sprinkle Pixie Dust

My G Love

Got to Go

Meat and Potatoes

Please Just Start

Kiss Me Goodnight

Where's Your Backbone

IT'S PUPPY LOVE

Pros and Cons

Lovie's Lazy Lasagna

Momma Marie's Meatballs

Rise and Shine

Dance Party Music

It's Highly Suggested

Slowly but Surely

Roll with It

I'm Outta Here

Snuggles and Smooches

Prepare to Indulge

Reel It In

Stop the Insanity

Now or Never

Gone Too Far

Change Your Mind

Follow the Rules

Unfollow the Rules

Make the Changes

Lean in Closer

Bacon and Eggs

Throw a Party

Tell the Truth

Tell Me More

That's Just Wrong

Make It Right

It'll Get Better

Because of You

It's My Favorite

Very Worth It

Back off B*tch

Heart to Heart

I Do Remember

High School Reunion

Please Don't Leave

I Won't Forget

I Promise You

I Need Time

Comfort and Joy

The Little Things

Macaroni and Cheese

You're a Rockstar

Remember That Time

With Three Splenda

Pray Your Way

Dip into It

I'm Totally Sure

Extra Cheese Pizza

It Shall Pass

You're an As*hole

Over and Over

You're More Than

Driving Miss Daisy

You're Doing Great

Hop Skip Jump

Juicy Jersey Tomatoes

Mum's the Word

Sweet and Sassy

Jump for Joy

You Ugly Liar

You Do You

They're So Laughable

Stop the Abuse

Start Over Again

I Crave Comfort

Sprinkles on Top

Embrace Your Fears

Please and Thanks

On Garlic Bread

Look How Cute

Talk with Me

Chicken Parmesan Meatballs

The Sweetest Devotion

Make an Offer

Splashes of Happy

Have the Conversation

Update Your Preferences

That Really Hurt

Spend More Time

I Want This

I Need This

It's All You

It's All Yours

I Don't Care

I Don't Mind

Spaghetti and Meatballs

It's 5:00 Somewhere

Not My Style

I'm Forever Grateful

Fried Green Tomatoes

You're Too Funny

They're Better Frozen

Take the Plunge

Walk the Walk

Milk and Cookies

That's an Oxymoron

Will and Grace

Life in Pieces

Here We Are

I Always Wish

Always Beside You

Sweet and Sour

I Love Lucy

Act as If

Just Do It

When Pigs Fly

Don't Stop Believing

Not Today Satan

Make Yourself Glow

Sweet Pink Lemonade

Don't Go There

Make It Better

Drinks All Around

Blaze of Glory

Where Was I

Go F*ck Yourself

Who Asked You

White Cheddar Ranch

Chocolate Covered Everything

Couldn't Help Myself

Learn the Lesson

It Does Matter

Honey Do List

Piping Hot Pizza

Make More Choices

It is Important

This is Christmas

Whatever Works Best

Puppy Breath Smell

Warm Baked Cookies

Ice Cold Beverages

Pick Your Poison

There's No Reason

Embrace Mini Moments

Give Second Chances

Play It Cool

Floss Your Teeth

Stop Drop Roll

Don't Be Afraid

Go in Peace

God Bless You

Carry Your Part

Be the Adult

Listening Means Everything

Exercise Your Soul

Think Big Thoughts

Wait Your Turn

Take a Stand

Watch Your Step

Keep Your Distance

Shut Your Piehole

God Bless America

Ask the Questions

Value All Life

Oldies but Goodies

You are Remembered

Laugh with Friends

Bottle of Wine

Extra Cheese Please

Consider the Source

Live Laugh Love

Admit Your Mistakes

Don't Remain Angry

Don't Be Sad

It's About Them

Follow the Rainbow

Accept All Gifts

Listen and Learn

Smell the Roses

Hang in There

Words Are Art

Have Some Integrity

Say a Prayer

Watch Your Back

Believe in Miracles

Donate to Charity

Playtime is Underrated

Cherish and Treasure

Tootsie Roll Lollipops

Appreciate True Colors

Palm Trees Swaying

Crunchy French Fries

Tossing Joy Bombs

Lovie Loves You

We'll Talk Tomorrow

Light My Fire

Make the Call

Warm Balmy Breeze

Forgive and Forget

Note to Self

Applauding Dr. Rupp

Generous and Gracious

Clearwater Beach Florida

Get Really Curious

Realize Others' Value

Your Rose-colored Glasses

Heaven on Earth

The Perfect Storm

My New Favorite

Why Is It

Job Well Done

Bye Amateur Hour

Release Resolve Rejoice

It's Game Time

Be Done Fighting

Let Me Know

Make Happy Happen

Take More Chances

Dance More Dances

Not This Lifetime

Dungeness Crab Legs

Extra Melted Butter

Magnificent Marvelous Millie

While Dozing Off

In the Meantime

Books are Magic

Get a Life

Laugh at Yourself

Stop the Can't

Eat with Gusto

Raise Your Glass

Sweet Smelling Rain

On My Own

Just Keep Chugging

The Sweetest Peach

Shine Your Light

It's Happy Hour

Five More Minutes

Keep in Touch

Sense of Self

Make Your Day

The Madness Begins

Whatever It Takes

Where Am I

Turn the Page

Let's Do This

I've Been Thinking

Unpack Your Baggage

Have a Seat

Go Chill Out

MY NEXT LIFE

BEING GRACIE GIRL

Shaken and Stirred

Beaming Bright Light

This One Morning

A Day Late

A Dollar Short

Lost My Marbles

Have a Heart

In This Moment

Ice Cream Sandwich

It's Like This

Skies of Blue

Safe Than Sorry

Sh*ts and Giggles

Create Your Space

Sneaky Little F*cks

Keep Yourself Honest

Don't Fade Away

Golden Stardust Sprinkles

I Must Answer

Nuggets of Wisdom

Here's the Scoop

World of Good

Burst Your Bubble

Don't Get Discouraged

That Was Easy

Why Not Now

So Worth It

Buy the Shoes

Enjoy the Company

Just Be You

Eat the Cake

Ask for Help

Follow Your Heart

Give Yourself Time

One Hit Wonder

Precious and Priceless

Tried and True

Stop Your Smothering

Remember Being You

You're No Better

Do You Understand

Yes to You

Shine on Lovelies

Your Beautiful Eyes

Wonderful and Wise

Where Are You

Always Show Up

Fly High Freebird

I Dare You

Let's Face It

In This Together

Chin Up Buttercup

Be That Person

Say Your Peace

Back-up Band Singer

Parmesan Garlic Wings

You Slay Me

Way Back When

Let's Meet Halfway

What the F*ck

Extra Extra Crispy

Pick It Up

Spring is Here

Make It Happen

Light the Path

Sing the Song

Turn It Around

Hold on Tight

With or Without

Take a Nap

Get Some Sleep

Color Your World

Here It Comes

Life Goes On

Love Sunny Days

Do unto Others

Cheesesteak Fried Onions

Best Hugger Ever

Tell Your Story

Sleep Dream Repeat

Never Let Go

Thanks for Asking

It's My Thing

Popcorn with Butter

Make It Stop

I Just Can't

Down the Shore

You're the Best

Mom was Right

Visualize Throat Punching

Friends and Family

Down to Earth

On the Beach

You Shouldn't Have

Open Your Eyes

Flip the Coin

Bonfires and Beaches

Arms Wide Open

Keep the Change

New Year's Day

Share It All

Chicken Chow Mein

A Quiet Morning

Goodness Grace Us

Bunch of Clowns

Famous Last Words

Told You So

A Walk Outside

Not My Business

A Good Workout

Love Loving Yourself

Reflecting on Life

Roast Beef Sandwich

A Kitten's Purr

Imagine the Possibilities

Smiles All Around

Side of Pickles

Pomegranate Iced Tea

To the Left

To the Right

The Other Way

Would You Rather

Time to Practice

Just Try It

The Hokey Pokey

Love You Truly

Walk with Me

Your Wish List

The Foo Fighters

Sleeping Under Stars

You Be True

Smarter Than That

Hold My Hand

Rain or Shine

Stuck on Stupid

Dare to Dream

Keep It Real

Cheers to All

Thanks So Much

Welcome the Compliment

Someone Needs You

Melt My Heart

Good Better Best

Having It All

Oranges and Watermelon

No Strings Attached

Laughter Works Wonders

Seize the Day

A Different Perspective

That's F*cked Up

All About Comfort

Count Your Blessings

French Onion Soup

Happily Ever After

The Rolling Stones

Do Your Best

Chocolate Covered Pretzels

Life is Beautiful

Celebrate the Win

Shot of Whiskey

No Shoes Required

Let It Be

When It's Love

Sad but True

Can't Be Serious

Tables Have Turned

Make My Day

Look at You

I Care Because

Let's Share Nachos

Sugar and Spice

Keep on Smiling

Take in Everything

No Matter What

Toss the Toxic

Give to Others

One Loyal Friend

Movie Date Night

Collect and Connect

Where's My Marbles

Nobody is Perfect

See the Good

Always Expect Less

Learn from Yesterday

Be Better Tomorrow

Summer is Spectacular

Be at Peace

My Best Friend

Reason to Believe

You Look Fabulous

My Heart's Broken

Shrimp Pasta Salad

Miss You Much

All About You

I'm Your Guido

Chocolate is Happiness

Be My Guest

Simply the Best

Please Be Quiet

Never Too Late

The First Snowfall

Not Now Please

Teeny Tiny Things

Little Too Late

One More Piece

Keep Sunshine Going

Philly Cheesesteak Wit

Practice the Pause

Sit with Me

Classic Rock Music

Philly Soft Pretzels

Expand Your Horizons

Cream Cheese Bagel

And That's Okay

Make Today Magical

Key Lime Moonshine

Divine Dark Chocolate

Dirty Rotten Bas*ards

I'm Always Here

Clams Mussels Shrimp

Dips and Chips

In Your Dreams

Sweet and Salty

Take Me Home

Lazy Brained People

Sound of Silence

Glitters of Gold

The Sweetest Thing

Irish Eyes Smiling

Omelet with Everything

In My Heart

Relax Your Mind

You Got It

Silence Speaks Volumes

Communicate Your Feelings

Chocolate Chip Cookies

In Due Time

Please Reach Out

You're Beyond Ridiculous

It's No Secret

Love Sweet Love

My Favorite Things

Just in Time

Open Door Policy

Dream Sweet Dreams

Nothing Equals Love

Change Your View

Faithfully Yours Forever

Give Yourself Permission

Don't Make Promises

Plays Well Together

Baby Back Ribs

Some Good News

You Never Know

You Never Will

WE NEED HOPE

Just in Case

Love You Most

Look at Me

It Isn't Over

Write the Book

Eat Pray Love

An Open Fire

All for You

Everyone Makes Mistakes

Every Last Word

Play for Keeps

Dead or Alive

My Happy Place

Just in Case

You're Utterly Ignorant

Touch One's Heart

Floor is Yours

Brooklyn Pizza Pie

Work in Progress

To be Honest

Inspire One Soul

Shut the Door

Hazelnut Coffee Flavor

Close the Door

Open Your Mind

Thanks for Listening

Encourage One Mind

Keep the Peace

It's Not You

Help Me Jesus

All in One

I Hate Ignorance

Join the Club

Ready Set Go

You're Absolutely Wonderful

No One Knows

Steak Medium Well

A Rollercoaster Ride

I Need Help

Pray for Hope

Pull It Off

Taken for Granted

Looking for Answers

Here I Am

Be the Cheeseboard

Grilled Chicken Caesar

Not Ready Yet

Keep a Secret

Sing Along Songs

I Was Broken

Life's Too Short

Always Be Kind

Keep Me Posted

Perfect Sunny Day

Remind Me Again

Light Your Fire

Make It Yours

That's for Me

Things Are Uncertain

Hazy Hot Humid

Something About You

Cheeseburger in Paradise

To Live Again

Did You Know

A Million Stars

Dreams in Color

Make Yourself Happy

We Aren't Together

Lemon Yellow Sun

Grab a Seat

Yippie Yi Yay

Definitely with Sprinkles

Not Sure Why

Rise Above Bulls*it

Never Fade Away

Brilliant Little Sunbeam

Break the Rules

Care to Care

Lift Someone Up

Who Are They

Sense of Belonging

Methods of Madness

Holly Jolly Christmas

Wounds to Wisdom

Won't Be Long

Loved That Moment

Wine and Cheese

Why Not Me

Good to Giggle

Always with Me

Stop Telling Lies

Pardon the Interruption

My Perfect Imperfections

Let Joy In

Long Story Short

One Split Second

One Single Moment

Sip Sip Hooray

Maybe They're Wrong

You Are Right

Have F*cking Fun

I Hear You

Your Inner Child

Gifts from Grief

How Sadly Pathetic

Anybody in There

There's Always Tomorrow

Then There's You

I Love Me

Oh It's You

Nineteenth Nervous Breakdown

Dreary to Cheery

Your Opinion Counts

Less is More

Bologna and Cheese

It's About Us

What a Mug

Coming to Terms

Change of Heart

Bubble Gum Bubbles

I Still Believe

Prove Me Wrong

Do Happy Things

Eventually is Now

Taking a Minute

You Know Better

The Last Time

Respect Yourself Enough

Watching Paint Dry

Please Don't Settle

Stone Cold Crazy

Memories Are Special

Sweet Summer Corn

Maybe Just Maybe

Beach and Boardwalk

Feed the Hungry

Best Case Scenario

Choose Very Carefully

The Grace Card

Days We Laughed

Times We Cried

Bed of Roses

You F*cking Knew

That's the Spirit

You Go Girl

Feel the Love

Over the Moon

Fat and Fabulous

Pause Your Piehole

Remember with Love

It's Long Overdue

Wish for Hope

You Ever Wonder

Yikes and Yowsa

Click to Give

Block the Ugly

Vanilla with Sprinkles

Whisper Sweet Nothings

Because I Said

You Cutie Patootie

Give More Than

My Little Loves

The Perfectly Imperfect

The Crockpot Queen

Whipped Buttercream Icing

Isn't It Lovely

My Whole World

It's the Weekend

What She Said

My Funny Valentine

Beach Dogs Chocolate

Feeling Hilariously Delirious

Riding the Wave

Warm Summer Nights

Heart and Soul

Tears of Joy

Chocolate and Vanilla

Keep It Together

A Child's Laughter

Vanilla Orange Creamsicle

A Baby's Giggle

Black and White

Ten Tiny Toes

A Warm Embrace

Saying It's Okay

I'll Have More

Safe and Sound

One Simple Note

In a Minute

One Kind Gesture

One More Please

You're the Bomb

You're Good People

Thin Mint Cookies

In Your Face

It's Nothing Personal

Sweetest Person Ever

That's a Wrap

Believe in Yourself

Just a Thought

Flea Market Finds

You Got This

From Your Lips

Play Nicely People

Oh Hell No

You're So Wrong

Take My Hand

Change the Channel

Thoughts Words Deeds

What a Crock

-60-

Many Blessings Ahead

Fall to Pieces

Take a Shift

All that's Gone

Repair Your Heart

The Quiet Moments

Acts of Kindness

Ask for It

It'll Never Change

It Must Change

Respect is Earned

Another Cannoli Please

Suntan Lotion Scent

Give Your All

Happy for You

More Love Letters

Not My Favorite

More or Less

Life Lessons Learned

Take Me Back

My Absolute Favorite

You're a Gem

I Scoop Poop

The Party's Over

Fresh Cut Grass

Cuddles and Snuggles

Walking the Dog

Before It Rains

Keep Good Friends

It Takes Nothing

WE NEED FAITH

Open Your Heart

Mom's Deviled Eggs

Life is Messy

Love Conquers All

Coffee First Please

You're So Vain

Imagine Life Without

Search Your Soul

Don't Underestimate Me

Your Eyes Only

Crashing Ocean Waves

Time After Time

Ice Cream Cake

French Onion Dip

Good Old Days

Hotter than Hell

You Heartless B*tch

Big Frosty Beer

Ignorance is Ugly

Love Your Smile

You Really Suck

Acknowledge and Appreciate

Lovie Loves Loyalty

Swimming with Dolphins

Happiest Happy Hour

Handsome Little Man

Cool Whip Recipes

Sweet White Peaches

Riddle Me This

Don't Stop Smiling

Cheeky Little Human

Bacon Eggs Cheese

Leave Heart Prints

Hang on Snoopy

Big Girl Panties

Your Eyes Sparkle

Creamy Alfredo Sauce

No One's Perfect

The Italian Market

Heartbreaking yet Heartwarming

What A Joke

Fake Phony F*ck

Keep on Laughing

Please Pay Attention

We Bleed Green

If You're Happy

Buck Up Buttercup

Bigger is Better

You Slay Me

You're Absolutely Wrong

Walking the Beach

Having Me Time

Make Wonderful Memories

What's More Important

Who's More Important

Love You More

Today Be Happy

Channel Your Fabulousness

Lying Two-Faced B*tch

Full of Sh*t

My Rizzi Love

Stars Twinkling Above

Write the Letter

Beautiful Baby Bella

It's a Wrap

Hop on Board

You and Me

The Calm Before

I'm Still Waiting

It's Not Okay

Create the Magic

I'm Still Standing

Mom's Mashed Potatoes

I'm Not Sorry

Which is Better

Little Baby Feet

Hide and Seek

Don't Give In

So Stinkin' Cute

Time to Shine

You Aren't Important

Lift Yourself Up

A Great Idea

You're So Exhausting

I'm Over It

You Should Leave

Plant a Garden

I'm a Beachaholic

Don't Embarrass Yourself

Fields of Wildflowers

Football Season Fan

Thanks A Million

To Be Frank

May I Digress

Anesthesia is Wonderful

I Want More

Bumming and Slumming

What's for Dinner

My Linnie Love

Philly Cream Cheese

Let's Get Together

Shimmy Yourself Happy

Shake it Off

Because I Care

Keep Yourself Lit

Sunrises and Sunsets

Dance Dance Dance

Hand Over Hand

All is Well

Ask About Me

A New Day

I'm Over You

On the Boardwalk

I'm Beyond Done

You Don't Say

Well Looky Here

The Great Pretender

Eat the Cupcakes

Thunder and Lightning

The Sweetest Sweetheart

Frozen Hershey Kisses

Furry Little Furballs

Over the Rainbow

Agree to Disagree

Movie and Popcorn

Bloom and Blossom

Frozen Rum Concoctions

The Greatest Comeback

So Not Funny

Here for This

Conversations and Cocktails

Turkey and Stuffing

You Are Loved

Frosty the Snowman

Never and Always

Libations for Everyone

Rock and Roll

Let It Be

A Mutual Understanding

Memories Last Forever

Comfy Cozy Clothes

You're My Sunshine

Be the Reason

Christmas Tree Ornaments

Auld Lang Syne

Never Gonna Happen

Garlic Buttered Salmon

Garlic on Everything

Miss You More

Hurts So Bad

See You Tomorrow

Home Sweet Home

Honey Roasted Pistachios

Worth Fighting For

Never Gets Old

Read My Lips

BBQ Spare Ribs

Not Worth It

Collect the Seashells

Taste the Snowflakes

Blow the Bubbles

Smile at Dogs

Laugh A Lot

Play the Lottery

We're Better Off

Fulfill Your Wishes

Cancel My Subscription

Give Yourself Credit

Shimmery Red Lipstick

Kentucky Fried Chicken

Breakfast for Dinner

Smile and Shine

Little Struggles Matter

Nothing is Wasted

Want for Nothing

Indian Summer Weather

Good for You

Go Roller Skating

And Most Importantly

Love Yourself Most

You're My Reminder

A Little Late

Shouldn't Couldn't Wouldn't

Little Side Humor

Chats and Chocolates

Roasted Garlic Sauce

Taco Stuffed Peppers

I Adore You

Become the Light

Better Days Ahead

Best Movie Ever

Lydia's French Toast

Pot of Gold

Short Stack Pancakes

Lucky for Us

People Exhaust Me

Poppy Seed Bagel

Take a Break

Four Leaf Clover

Faithful Fluffy Friends

Fresh Cut Flowers

Keep Yourself Alive

Sunkissed Summer Skin

Front Row Seats

Coffee Smells Delightful

The Bunny Hop

The Plot Thickens

You Bore Me

Greasy Boardwalk Pizza

Say You're Sorry

Don't Go Numb

All's I Know

Shame on You

Dummy Juice Drinker

Late Night Drives

Orange Cream Milkshake

Simmer Down Sally

Chocolate Frosted Donut

Live and Grin

Dunk the Oreo

Falling in Love

It's Last Call

Everybody Calm Down

No Fruit Please

Everyone Already Knows

Diet Decaf Tea

Who Says That

Who Does That

Crappy Sh*t Show

Jumping to Conclusions

Key West Florida

You're Absolutely Hilarious

Take the Pictures

Love Your Time

Your First Kiss

Yellow Brick Road

Crispy Fried Shrimp

Sunrise Beach Walk

Sunset Beach Walk

This Just In

WE NEED LOVE

Still Running Strong

You F*ck Cluster

Share Funny Stories

Mom and Dad

Living Wide Open

Discover Small Treasures

A Comforting Heartbeat

Crimson and Clover

Learn Something New

Flowers in Spring

Share Your Smile

Homemade Butter Cookies

Be Beautiful You

Dare to Share

In Another Lifetime

Embrace the Uncertainty

Trust the Wait

Tomorrow Isn't Promised

Stairway to Heaven

Nothing is Certain

Bowl of Cheerios

Before You Leave

Reap the Rewards

Good Luck Charm

It's the Journey

Expect the Unexpected

She Was Wrong

Repeat After Me

Flat Out Lies

Hurts My Heart

Relax and Rewind

Don't Fear Failure

One Thousand Percent

Forget Me Not

Power of Calm

A Wonderful World

Help Me Remember

Turkey Cheese Hoagie

Tears Will Flow

Let Freedom Ring

It's About Integrity

Feed Your Happy

Fritos Corn Chips

Cheese Mushroom Omelet

Be Magically Marvelous

Give a S*it

No You Didn't

Be More Honest

Don't Be Uncool

Sun Sand Surf

In the Moonlight

The Humane Society

Coming Up Roses

Your Love Story

Champagne Ice Bucket

Seeing is Believing

For the Taking

Crunchy Dipsy Doodles

The New Normal

My Oh My

Piece of Cake

Icing on Top

Happiest of Birthdays

Fat Lady Sang

Spread the Word

Keep It Happy

Easy Sunday Morning

Let It Happen

Celebrate Every Win

Weird and Wonderful

Light the Darkness

Warm the Cold

Keep Eating Cake

Your Belly Laugh

Everything's Different Now

Every Single Day

Razzle Dazzle Darling

Create WOW Moments

Do Not Disturb

Ooh La La

Hot Toasted Grinders

May Cause Goosebumps

Get a Clue

Silence is Golden

This is Everything

Soft Shell Crabs

Long Time Coming

Apologies Not Necessary

You're Very Welcome

Waves Crashing In

It's a Fact

Have Another One

Big Fluffy Clouds

I Love Visualizing

Take That Vacation

Please Don't Interrupt

I Call Bulls*it

I'm a Hopeaholic

Trial and Error

Doesn't Surprise Me

Pack a Picnic

Just Stop Already

Yes You Did

Your Favorite Recipes

My Thoughts Exactly

As They Say

Pretty Rosy Cheeks

Green Bean Casserole

Here nor There

Karma's a Bi*ch

Eat Dessert First

Simple and Sane

Yummy Rum Bum

Always a Reason

Don't Wait Celebrate

Thank You Jesus

It's Worth It

The Bright Direction

Be Happy Now

Not for Me

Paw to Heart

Lazy Rainy Days

Shiny and Bright

On Your Birthday

Be a Cheerleader

Tootles and Tallyho

Living Life Blahless

Here's a Suggestion

Not Sure Anymore

Talk is Cheap

Always Kiss Goodnight

Opening Christmas Presents

You're So Beautiful

Shake Things Up

You've Outdone Yourself

Basic Human Decency

Your Cold Heart

It's My Life

Make Snow Angels

You'll Never Understand

Please Do Better

It Was You

Gifts of Forgiveness

Acting and Doing

Help Me Understand

A Wonderful Life

Here's the Deal

Listen Very Closely

Keep Dreams Alive

Cucumber Ice Water

More Love Letters

For a Lifetime

Kindness is Cool

Release the Crazy

Sorry Not Sorry

Talk to Me

Partners in Crime

Hoping and Scoping

Change is Coming

Always Feel Comfortable

Outdoor Summer Concerts

The Big Day

Sun Moon Stars

How Could You

Make Yourself Stronger

Peppermint Candy Canes

Inhale and Exhale

Please Stop Lying

Adopt a Furbaby

Let Us Pray

No In Between

Save Someone's Life

All Opinions Count

Give Flying F*cks

Quirky is Funny

People to Remember

It's Party Time

Places of Beauty

Don't Stop Now

Grow Up Already

They're in Heaven

Watching Over You

Your Attention Please

It's Your Life

I'm With You

We're All In

There's the Door

Flowers Just Because

By the Way

Yes or No

Uncrap Your Life

I Got You

Joke's on You

Vulnerability is Strength

Realize and Recognize

FRIENDS BEING THERE

FOR EACH OTHER

Dear Beautiful You

Hubbles' Cooking Creations

Be Here Now

What Motivates You

Choose Yourself First

Jumping in Puddles

Hugs Dry Tears

Candles Light Darkness

Own Worst Enemy

Enjoy the Journey

It's Not Fair

Life is Good

Wrong is Wrong

Right is Right

Moira and Karen

Lobster and Scallops

Under the Circumstances

No Bake Cheesecake

As We Speak

Compassion and Empathy

Constipation Fits You

Give It Meaning

Intermissions are Needed

Genuinely Be You

Young at Heart

One Simple Question

Too Many Cowards

All Adults Here

Worrier to Warrior

You Are Brilliant

Disease to Please

Channel into Courage

Cancelling Your Bullsh*t

Enjoy the Joy

Pepperoni Garlic Knots

Brave and Bravo

Sparkle Shimmer Shine

On the Flipside

Savor Every Bite

Chug Chugging Along

Fairly Slightly Complicated

Prioritize Your Crazy

Jumpstart Your Joy

Happiness is Happening

I'm Beyond Words

Your Best Moments

My Heart Expands

A Walk Outdoors

A Great Workout

This Current Moment

Goodness Grace Us

Smile Big Anyway

Jalapeno Popper Happy

Mobile Margarita Bar

You Have Options

Choose Your Pain

Just One Minute

You've Got Class

Tropical Pineapple Schnapps

Cherish Handwritten Notes

Cheeky and Sassy

I'm Hopelessly Devoted

Another Day Begins

Cheers to You

Tomorrow Didn't Come

Mom's Knocky Knees

Psychic or Psycho

Pity Party Cancelled

Service Over Self-Importance

Best Song Ever

Feed Your Cravings

Do You Care

Your Darkest Moment

Why Do They

Color My World

This is Magical

I'm Done Fighting

Don't Care Anymore

Know Your Worth

Unbelievable Joys Await

No Thank You

Winds of Winter

A Million Thoughts

A Gorgeous Soul

Happy Heavenly Birthday

Vodka Infused Watermelon

Happy Not Snappy

Bargain Basement Deals

Pay Your Respects

I Don't Understand

Dump the Don'ts

Celebrate Good Times

Moment of Truth

Dead End Job

Free Prize Inside

Garlic Crab Risotto

Never Say Diet

A Known Fact

They All Lie

Summertime Lightning Bugs

Never Stop Laughing

So Deeply Missed

I'll Never Again

Grilled Baked Barbequed

Smorgasbord of Seafood

Was Always You

For the Better

Leftover Chinese Food

You Have Nerve

More than Tired

It's Too Much

Grandmom's Chocolate Cake

Room to Roam

Priceless Precious Occasions

Treat Yourself Worthy

The Last Laugh

More Lobster Please

Dreams of You

You're So Important

Love is Everlasting

Doesn't Phase Me

White Garlic Pizza

I Miss Me

Rum Runner Slurpee

I'm So Ready

In My Thoughts

From Heaven Above

Apparently I'm Delusional

Guilty as Charged

Not Without You

Appreciate True Connections

Ray of Sunshine

A Falling Star

A Rainy Day

Your Favorite Book

Chocolate Chip Muffin

Matters to Me

Truer Than True

Catch Your Breath

You're the One

Sunny Side Up

So Not You

It's Really Them

There's That Smile

It's Game Changing

Make a "U"-turn

For the Love

If You Insist

Chocolate and Cheese

Darling Adorable Dimples

You're Very Mistaken

Recover Your Spirit

Piece of Work

Watermelon Ice Water

Until the End

Christmas Butter Cookies

Celebrate Your Successes

Please Just Stop

You Don't Know

It's Wishful Drinking

Grilled Cheese Anything

You Were Wrong

Doesn't Matter Anymore

Being Happy Matters

Stop Hurting People

Heart of Gold

There's Always Towanda

Appreciate the Moments

Work Your Magic

In My Dreams

Most Favorite Movie

Make the Time

Here There Everywhere

They Don't Care

Late Night Snacks

Can't Fix Stupid

Close Your Eyes

No Do Overs

Knock Yourself Out

Please Go Away

CALLING ON ANGELS

Good or Bad

Stop Kissing A*s

Times Like These

Bulls*it Free Zone

Just for You

Love Puppy Breath

Christmas in July

Calling All Angels

She Was Tired

She Was Weary

She Was Worried

But Not Anymore

It's Always Something

So Happy Together

Brand Spanking New

Never Say Goodbye

Hold onto Friends

Much Better Than

Before This Ends

They Got You

There's Always One

I'm All Ears

Yeah OK Whatever

Hope Over Hate

In Good Company

Makes Me Smile

Most Happy Day

You Should Care

Best Feeling Ever

You Are Garbage

By Appointment Only

No I Wasn't

Stay in Touch

Angels in Heaven

Angels on Earth

Delightful and Delicious

My Heart Hurts

Keep the Connection

Don't Lose Yourself

Own Your S*it

I'm Really Tired

Sesame Seed Bagel

Jiggle Your Wiggle

Make It Magical

Hello Wonderful You

Today's the Day

What's for Dessert

Place of Calm

Do for Others

You've Got Heart

Count Me In

You're Always Enough

Bring It On

Have Beautiful Dreams

Value Your Time

You're Better Than

Get Cozy Comfy

Give Goodnight Kisses

Sleep Well Friends

Dreams Come True

Here's some space to scribble down "three little words" that mean something to you. Have fun with it. Go crazy with it. Enjoy doing it. Knock it out of the park... 😊

_____

_____

_____

_____

_____

_____

_____

_____

_____

And Above All

Written with Love

From my Heart

I Appreciate You

And Sending A

BIGGER THAN BIG

This is me chilling out at a nearby river. I am most at peace and at my best when there's a body of water; more so when it's the beach, bay or ocean waters. It's a whole other lovely world for me!

I sat there on that bench to relax and think about some of my favorite things like the shore, laughter, loyalty, friends, music, breakfast, connections, love, animals, sunrises, sunsets, my angels in heaven (and here on earth). And I realized, it's not all about how much or how many, **it's all about how happy!**